TOOL KIT

DIG AND DUMP

Patty Whitehouse

Rourke
Publishing LLC
Vero Beach, Florida 32964

www.rourkepublishing.com

PHOTO CREDITS: © Armentrout: pages 6, 8, 9, 11, 12, 13, 18; © PIR: pages 4, 14; © Craig Lopetz: page 19; © constructionphotos.com: pages 5, 7, 17; © Ikemilai: page 10; © Sterger: page 15; © Andy Kazie: page 20; © kwerry: page 21; © pkruger: page 22

Editor: Robert Stengard-Olliges

Cover design by Nicola Stratford

Library of Congress Cataloging-in-Publication Data

Whitehouse, Patricia, 1958-
  Dig and dump / Patty Whitehouse.
      p. cm. -- (Tool kit)
  Includes index.
  ISBN 1-60044-207-2 (hardcover)
  ISBN 1-59515-564-3 (softcover)
  1. Excavation--Juvenile literature. 2. Shovels--Juvenile literature.
I. Title. II. Series: Whitehouse,
Patricia, 1958- Tool kit.
  TA732.W4785 2007
  624.1/52 22

Printed in the USA

CG/CG

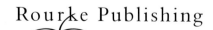

Rourke Publishing

www.rourkepublishing.com – sales@rourkepublishing.com
Post Office Box 3328, Vero Beach, FL 32964

Table of Contents

Digging and Dumping

This is a hole at a construction site. It was made with a digging **tool**.

Some holes need filling. Workers need to use a tool that dumps.

Tools For Work

Tools help with many kinds of work. Some tools are for building. Other tools are for growing things.

This book shows tools that dig and tools that dump.

Shovels and Spades

Shovels and spades are digging tools. A shovel has a scooped **blade**. A spade has a flat blade.

Workers use spades to dig holes in dirt or sand. They use shovels to scoop up dirt, sand, or other things.

Wheelbarrows

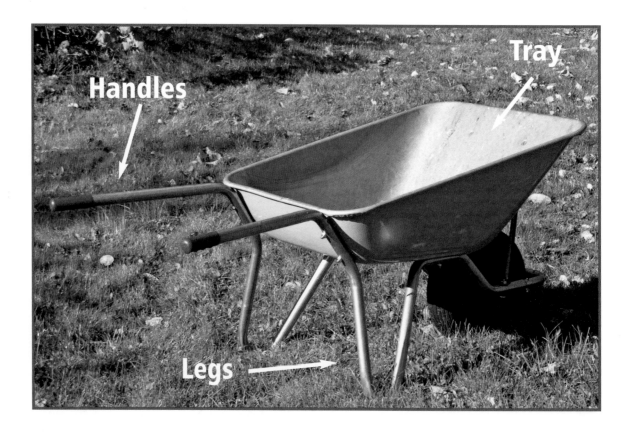

Wheelbarrows are dumping tools. Workers fill the tray with what they want to dump.

The wheel on the wheelbarrow makes it easy to move. A worker dumps it out by lifting the **handles**.

Post Hole Diggers

A post hole digger is a digging tool. It looks like two shovels hooked together.

Workers use post hole diggers to make deep holes. The holes are for posts for fences or stairs.

Cement Mixers

Cement mixers are dumping tools. They mix cement and hold it until it is ready to dump.

Cement

Cement is poured into a hole. It hardens and holds the fire hydrant in place.

Excavators and Bulldozers

Cab

Excavators are diggers. They are big machines that dig dirt. A worker controls the excavator from the cab.

Bucket

Bulldozers can dig and dump. They are big machines that dig dirt. They move dirt in a big bucket.

Dump Trucks

Dump trucks are dumpers. They get filled with dirt, rocks, or other things. Then they drive away.

The dump truck bed lifts up. The back gate opens.
The dirt or rocks dumps out.

Small Diggers and Big Diggers

This is a front loader. A front loader is a small machine. It has a bucket that scoops dirt.

This is a dragline excavator. It is a very big machine. It is bigger than a house.

Tool Safety

You should have an adult help you with any tools. You should wear gloves and goggles to protect yourself.

GLOSSARY

blade (BLAYD) — sharp part of a tool

cement (suh MENT) — mixture of powdered rocks and water used for making sidewalks and roads

excavator (EK skuh va ter) — a big machine that digs or moves dirt

handle (HAN duhl) — the part of a tool that is heldyou hold

tool (TOOL) — something that helps people do work

INDEX

FURTHER READING

Connor, Leslie. *Miss Bridie Chose A Shovel.* Houghton Mifflin; New York, 2004.

Miller, Heather. *Construction Worker.* Heinemann: Chicago, 2002.

Williams, Linda D. *Bulldozers.* Capstone Press: Mankato, MN, 2004.

WEBSITES TO VISIT

science.howstuffworks.com/engineering-channel.html
www.bobthebuilder.com/usa/index.html

ABOUT THE AUTHOR

Patty Whitehouse has been a teacher for 17 years. She is currently a Lead Science teacher in Chicago, where she lives with her husband and two teenage children. She enjoys reading, gardening, and writing about science for children.